AF269737

TAYLOR
SWIFT
UNSTOPPABLE
ICON

TAYLOR SWIFT

UNSTOPPABLE ICON

Marie-Therese Miller

LERNER PUBLICATIONS ◆ MINNEAPOLIS

Lerner Publications Company
An imprint of Lerner Publishing Group, Inc.
241 First Avenue North
Minneapolis, MN 55401 USA

For reading levels and more information, look up this title at www.lernerbooks.com.

Main body text set in Rotis Serif Std 55 Regular. Typeface provided by Adobe Systems.

Library of Congress Cataloging-in-Publication Data

Names: Miller, Marie-Therese, author.
Title: Taylor Swift : unstoppable icon / Marie-Therese Miller.
Description: Minneapolis, MN : Lerner Publications, 2025. | Series: Gateway biographies |
   Includes bibliographical references and index. | Audience: Ages 9–14 | Audience: Grades
   4–6 | Summary: "Taylor Swift isn't just a world-class musician—she's also a trendsetter,
   an entrepreneur, and an activist. From releasing her first album in 2006 to completing her
   record-breaking Eras Tour in 2024, readers will learn about her life." – Provided by publisher.
   Identifiers: LCCN 2024024054 (print) | LCCN 2024024055 (ebook) | ISBN 9798765649152
   (library binding) | ISBN 9798765661819 (paperback) | ISBN 9798765654798 (epub)
Subjects: LCSH: Swift, Taylor, 1989-–Juvenile literature. | Singers–United States–Biography–
   Juvenile literature. | Country musicians–United States–Biography–Juvenile literature.
Classification: LCC ML3930.S989 M57 2025 (print) | LCC ML3930.S989 (ebook) | DDC
   782.421642092 [B]–dc23/eng/20240528

LC record available at https://lccn.loc.gov/2024024054
LC ebook record available at https://lccn.loc.gov/2024024055

Manufactured in the United States of America
1-1011061-53495-8/14/2024

TABLE OF CONTENTS

Taylor Swift gives a star-studded performance in the rain on May 20, 2023, at Gillette Stadium.

Musical sensation Taylor Swift always puts on a good performance. Her May 20, 2023, concert at Gillette Stadium in Foxborough, Massachusetts, was no exception. Swift performed for more than three hours in the pouring rain. She began the concert with songs from her *Lover* era. Then she shook things up with songs from her albums *Fearless*, *Folklore*, and more. Swift gave it her all!

Devoted fans, or Swifties, skipped work, school, and even their graduation ceremonies to attend the concert. They dressed in outfits that represented Swift's albums. More than sixty-five thousand fans got drenched, but they sang loudly and cheered. After the show, Swift shared a few words about the concert. "We've had rain shows at Gillette Stadium before, but this was a full-on deluge that never let up," she said. "I just want to thank that iconic crowd!"

The concert at Gillette Stadium was just one stop on Swift's worldwide Eras Tour. It had been five years since her last world tour, and Swift wanted to go all out in her performances. She wanted to include music from all

Swift performs onstage for an Eras Tour concert in Dublin, Ireland, in June 2024.

her studio albums, or "eras" of her music. To prepare for the physical demands of touring, Swift began intense gym workouts six months beforehand to build her strength and stamina. She also worked with her choreographer to make sure the dance sections were just right.

All her preparations were worth it. The concerts were spectacular with atmospheric sets, stellar costumes, and more. At one point, special effects even made it look as though Swift was diving into a pool of water. The tour went on break in November 2023, with more dates in 2024. Fans and critics alike considered Swift's Eras Tour a resounding success. It was a triumph for Swift—with so much more to come.

TAYLOR'S EARLY LIFE

Taylor Alison Swift was born on December 13, 1989, in Reading, Pennsylvania. Her dad, Scott Kingsley Swift, was a financial adviser. Her mom, Andrea Gardner Swift, was a marketing executive. After having Taylor, Andrea decided to become a stay-at-home mom.

Taylor and her family lived on a Christmas tree farm in Cumru Township, Pennsylvania. Taylor's younger brother, Austin, was born just a few years after Taylor on March 11, 1992. Taylor remembers playing among the trees and sledding across the snow on the farm. The farm also had horses. Taylor rode horses competitively until she was twelve.

Taylor developed a love for writing when she began elementary school at Wyndcroft School in Pottstown, Pennsylvania. According to Barbara Kolvek, Taylor's elementary school music teacher, "She always was writing poetry, always. Even in music class, even when she shouldn't." Taylor did all kinds of writing. She wrote stories, poetry, and diary entries. She even won a national poetry contest when she was in fourth grade. Her winning poem was called "A Monster in My Closet!"

In 1999 Taylor's family moved to Wyomissing, Pennsylvania. There, she finished elementary school at West Reading Elementary Center. Around this time, Taylor became interested in singing and acting onstage. Musical talent ran in the family. Taylor's maternal grandmother, Marjorie Finlay, was a professional opera singer. Finlay traveled all over the world for her musical career. She inspired Taylor to pursue music.

When she was nine years old, Taylor joined Berks Youth Theatre Academy. She performed in musicals such as *Annie, Grease, The Sound of Music*, and *Bye, Bye, Birdie.* Taylor even took singing and acting lessons in New York City. Singing was her passion. She was seriously considering a future career in music and wondered which musical direction she should take.

Taylor was a huge fan of country music. She decided this style of music was a natural fit for her. She loved to listen to country artists. Shania Twain and LeAnn Rimes were two of her favorite female country singers. Taylor

A Shark and a Novel

Growing up, Taylor's family owned a vacation home in Stone Harbor, New Jersey. She spent summers there from when she was two until she was fourteen. Her summers were filled with adventures in the sand and water. The family's vacation home was on Sanctuary Bay. Living so close to the bay, Taylor encountered ocean wildlife. "One time a dolphin swam into our basin," she said. "We had a family of otters who would live on our deck at night." One summer a shark washed up on the dock. Taylor was too afraid to swim after that. Instead, she stayed inside and wrote a novel.

In 2011 Swift got to be in a video for the Country Music Television Awards with one of her idols, Shania Twain (*right*).

began singing covers, or versions of other performers' country songs. Her dream was to one day have a recording deal.

When she was eleven years old, she made a demo, or a recording, of these covers. During spring break, Taylor, her mother, and Austin traveled to Nashville, Tennessee, the heart of the country music industry. While her mom and brother stayed in the car, Taylor walked up and down Music Row, a district in downtown Nashville famous for record labels, publishing houses, recording studios, and more. She left her demos at the front desks of record companies.

At the time, Taylor had no experience with record companies and didn't know there was an official process to getting signed. She told them, "Hi, I'm Taylor. I'm eleven. I want a record deal. Call me." She didn't get any deals. Only one person responded to her to explain that this wasn't how they did things. Instead of feeling discouraged by the experience, the rejection only strengthened Taylor's desire to work harder.

SiGNiNG RECORD DEaLS

Taylor's first step toward getting a record deal was learning how to play the guitar. She began taking guitar lessons at the age of twelve. She worked hard to improve her guitar-playing skills. She practiced so many hours on her twelve-string guitar that her fingers bled and became calloused. Taylor also started writing her own lyrics and music. The first song she wrote was "Lucky You." She wrote many songs about romantic relationships and heartbreak even though she hadn't yet experienced these things. She drew inspiration from characters in books and movies for those lyrics.

At this time, Taylor arranged to sing in front of people whenever she had the chance. She sang karaoke at different venues. She performed at festivals and sang the national anthem at sporting events. In April 2002, Taylor sang the "Star-Spangled Banner" at a Philadelphia 76ers pro basketball game. Later that year, she performed the national anthem at the US Open, a tournament for pro tennis players.

At thirteen, she returned to Music Row with songs she had written herself. She was more successful this time.

RCA Records signed her to a development deal. But a year later, when it was time to renew her contract, she decided to leave. RCA wanted her to record songs that other people wrote, but Taylor wanted to record songs that she wrote.

When Taylor was fourteen, she convinced her parents to move to Tennessee. The move would make it easier for her to pursue her musical career. Her dad got a job transfer to Tennessee, and the family purchased a house

Swift with songwriter Liz Rose (*right*) at the 2010 Grammy Awards

in Hendersonville, which is close to Nashville. Taylor attended Hendersonville High School. That same year, she signed a songwriting contract with Sony/ATV Music Publishing. She was the youngest person to sign with the company. After school, Taylor usually wrote songs. She often worked with songwriter Liz Rose, who would eventually write songs for artists such as Carrie Underwood, Little Big Town, and more.

Swift returns to her roots in 2018 and performs at the Bluebird Cafe with country musician Craig Wiseman (*left*).

Taylor later performed at a songwriters showcase at the Bluebird Cafe in Nashville. There, she caught the attention of record executive Scott Borchetta, who was in the audience. He was about to start his own record company, Big Machine Records. He asked Taylor if she would sign with his new company when it was up and running. Borchetta would allow Taylor to record her own songs. She agreed and signed with Big Machine Records in 2005.

A COUNTRY ARTIST

Swift released her debut album, self-titled *Taylor Swift*, on October 24, 2006. She was only sixteen when the country album dropped. The song "Tim McGraw" had been released as the album's first single in the summer of 2006. The song is about young love and the heartbreak of losing that love. It reached number forty on the *Billboard* Hot 100. The album also includes other hit songs such as "Teardrops on My Guitar" and "Should've Said No."

Another song on the album is "Our Song." Swift originally wrote this song for her ninth-grade talent show. This song was number one on *Billboard*'s Hot 100 Country Songs and made Swift the youngest artist to write and perform a number one country song.

From the start, Swift's lyrics seemed as if they were coming directly from her diary. She drew from her personal experiences and emotions to write her lyrics. She also had a talent for engaging storytelling. Journalist Jack Dickey said, "[Swift] writes . . . with a poet's delicate touch and a dramatist's nose for conflict."

With her first album, Swift started to form a close connection

Swift rehearses onstage for the 2007 Academy of Country Music Awards.

with her fans that would continue throughout her career. According to Swift, she "decided to encode the lyrics with hidden messages using capital letters." She would leave "Easter eggs," or hidden clues, for her fans to discover and decipher. Fans might spot them in her album notes, videos, and even in her costumes. Swift also used the social media platform Myspace to keep in touch with her fans.

After her debut album was released, Swift needed a flexible school schedule to tour. She transferred from Hendersonville High School to Aaron Academy for a homeschool program. Swift performed as an opening act for many artists, including Rascal Flatts, George Strait, Brad Paisley, Faith Hill, and even Tim McGraw—the artist she named her first single after.

Swift released her second studio album, *Fearless*, on November 11, 2008. This country album also appealed to some pop fans. The album includes the hit songs "Love Story," which

Swift signing an autograph for a fan on the red carpet

With an elaborate castle set, Swift performs her song "Love Story" at the 2008 Country Music Association Awards.

was inspired by the play *Romeo and Juliet*; "You Belong with Me"; and "The Best Day," a tribute to Swift's close relationship with her mother. On April 23, 2009, Swift was ready for her first solo tour and launched the Fearless Tour.

Swift's career also expanded into the movie industry. For example, she played a small role in the film *Hannah*

Swift performs at Madison Square Garden as part of her Fearless Tour in 2009.

Montana: The Movie, where she sang her song "Crazier." She also wrote a song for the movie's soundtrack called "You'll Always Find Your Way Back Home."

On September 13, 2009, Swift attended the MTV Video Music Awards. She won the Best Female Video award for "You Belong with Me." She was only a few lines into her acceptance speech when rapper Kanye West jumped up onstage and grabbed the microphone. He insisted that Beyoncé should have won this award instead. Swift was confused and shocked by the interruption and didn't finish her speech. The audience booed West. But in the confusion, Swift thought they were booing her. Later that night, Beyoncé won the Video of the Year award and invited Swift onstage to finish her acceptance speech.

Swift won many other awards for *Fearless*, including the 2009 Country Music Association's award for Music Video of the Year. Then, in 2010, Swift won four Grammy Awards, including the Grammy for Best Country Album. She also won the Grammy for Album of the Year. At just twenty, Swift was the youngest person at the time to win that award.

Not everything was wonderful for Swift at the 2010 Grammys. She performed the song "Today Was a Fairytale." She sang off-key, possibly because of a technical

Swift takes home a whopping four awards at the 2009 Country Music Association Awards.

Swift giving an acceptance speech for winning the Grammy for Album of the Year in 2010

issue that meant Swift couldn't hear the music very well. In a harsh review of her performance, music critic Bob Lefsetz said that she should have used auto-tune to correct the pitch of her voice.

Swift would later write a song called "Mean" that is likely aimed at Lefsetz. The song appears on her third studio album, *Speak Now*, which was released on

October 25, 2010. She wrote every song on this album without any cowriters. Swift often writes songs about the relationships and breakups she has experienced without mentioning the subject of the songs. Fans believe some songs on *Speak Now*, such as "Dear John" and "Back to December," are about Swift's former relationships.

Swift soon went on tour again, this time for *Speak Now*. The Speak Now World Tour ran from February 2011 to March 2012. Big Machine also released a documentary of the tour called *Speak Now: World Tour Live* on November 21, 2011.

Swift performing at Madison Square Garden in November 2011 for her Speak Now World Tour

POPPING OVER

Slowly, Swift's music was moving from country to pop. Her album *Red* was released on October 22, 2012, and was a mix of both genres. Swift sings about taking a chance on a risky romance in her hit song "I Knew You Were Trouble." The catchy breakup song "We Are Never Ever Getting Back Together" reached number one on the *Billboard* Hot 100.

"All Too Well" also spent a week on the *Billboard* chart, and it remains one of Swift's favorite songs on the album. It recalls the story of a love affair that has ended. Swift noted that the song begins in fall, her

A Smart Businessperson

Over the years, Swift has partnered with many brands. From 2011 until 2014, she designed her own fragrance line with Elizabeth Arden, a cosmetic company. In 2012 she partnered with Keds, a sneaker company, in a multiyear contract to sell their shoes. She later collaborated with Diet Coke in 2013, becoming a brand ambassador to help promote their beverage. She also offered exclusive album releases through Target.

Swift singing songs from her album *Red* at a performance in London, England

favorite season. It includes memorable imagery, such as dancing by the refrigerator light, and a red scarf, which symbolizes love and longing for a lost love.

Between albums, Swift found time for other projects. She voiced the character Audrey in the 2012 animated movie *The Lorax*. Swift also wrote two songs, "Safe and Sound" and "Eyes Open," for the soundtrack of the 2012 movie adaptation of *The Hunger Games*. She would later play the part of Rosemary in the 2014 movie *The Giver*.

Then the time came to take *Red*'s songs on tour. Swift's Red Tour ran from March 2013 to June 2014. But while on tour, an incident happened in June 2013. Swift held a backstage meet and greet with fans in Denver, Colorado.

While having his photo taken with Swift, local radio DJ David Mueller groped her. Swift was horrified. Her team told Mueller's boss about the incident, and he was fired from his job. But the fallout from the incident didn't stop there.

In 2015 Mueller sued Swift for nearly $3 million in damages. He said he was fired based on her false allegations. In return, Swift countersued him for the assault for a symbolic $1. According to Swift's attorney, she did not want money from Mueller. She wanted to send a message about Mueller's wrongful actions. In an interview, Swift stated that if Mueller was bold enough to assault her in a room full of people, she was worried about what he might do to other young women. Swift eventually won her countersuit in 2017.

Before the release of her fifth studio album in October 2014, Swift met with fans in Secret Sessions. She welcomed them to her homes in New York City; Rhode Island;

Swift makes a stop in Philadelphia, Pennsylvania, on her Red Tour in July 2013 and performs at Lincoln Financial Field.

Swift sings songs from her album *1989* at MetLife Stadium in East Rutherford, New Jersey.

Los Angeles, California; and Nashville. There, fans listened to the new album and ate cookies Swift baked for them. Then, on October 27, 2014, Swift released *1989*. With this album, she broke completely away from country music and embraced pop. She even decided not to attend any of the country music awards to confirm her departure from the genre.

The album includes the song "Blank Space," in which Swift pokes fun at her reputation for having many romantic relationships. It spent a whopping seven weeks at number one on *Billboard*'s Hot 100! The album's hit song "Shake It Off" is a catchy song about not letting criticism drag you down, and it spent four weeks at number one.

But Swift faced criticism for her "Shake It Off" music video. In the video, she performs a variety of dance styles

Spotify and Apple

In November 2014, Taylor Swift took her music down from Spotify. Her position was that musical artists should be paid whenever their music is played. This went against Spotify's terms at the time, which allowed people to listen to songs for free with ads. Swift claimed this wasn't fair to artists. A year later, Swift also confronted Apple Music about not paying artists royalties during its free trial streaming period. Apple eventually changed its policy, so she kept her music on its platform. Spotify modified its policy very little, but as more fans asked to hear her music on the platform, Swift changed her mind. She put all her music back on Spotify on June 9, 2017.

from ballet to breakdancing to hip-hop. At one point, Swift crawls through the legs of a Black woman, who is twerking. Critics accused Swift of appropriating Black culture and racial stereotyping in this video. Swift did not comment on these criticisms, but the video's director, Mark Romanek, defended the video as inclusive. He also said it was satire that played with many music video tropes, clichés, and stereotypes.

Once more, Swift went on the road for her fans. The 1989 World Tour ran from May to December 2015. Later, in February 2016, Swift's album *1989* won the Grammy for the Best Pop Vocal Album. She also won for Best Album of the Year. She is the first woman to win that award twice.

Taking a Stand

In 2016 Swift's feud with West resumed and expanded to include West's then wife, Kim Kardashian. West released a song that called Swift a derogatory name. Swift was unhappy with the lyric. In response, Kardashian posted an audio tape on social media that had Swift allegedly agreeing to the lyric, but Swift insisted the tape was edited. Then Kardashian labeled Swift a snake on social media. Fans of Kardashian and West proceeded to target Swift. After this, Swift stayed largely out of the public view for a year.

A few months later, Swift released her sixth album,

Swift performs at the 2017 Jingle Ball at Madison Square Garden in New York City.

Reputation, on November 10, 2017. It includes "Look What You Made Me Do," a song about getting even. The song's music video features snake images, which led many people to believe this song was about Kardashian and West. Swift took the album on the road for her Reputation Stadium Tour from May to November 2018.

Around that time, a major event was happening in Swift's life. Her contract with Big Machine Records was expiring in November 2018. But the contract she signed didn't give her the copyrights to her master recordings, or original recordings, of all the songs on her first six albums. Owning the copyright to a master recording is important for singers. This gives them the legal right to license the recording, such as for TV shows, film, and commercials. Without owning the masters, artists have no legal right over those versions of their work.

When record executive Scooter Braun purchased Big Machine Records in June 2019, Swift tried to buy the rights to her masters without success. Singer Kelly Clarkson suggested that Swift rerecord those six albums. Although that was a massive amount of work, Swift decided it was worth the effort to do some rerecording to regain control of her music. She later rerecorded *Fearless*, *Red*, *Speak Now*, and *1989*, adding *(Taylor's Version)* to all the titles. The new albums have special tracks to encourage fans to buy them.

Swift made sure that the next contract she signed allowed her to keep the rights to her masters. Following the expiration of her contract with Big Machine, she signed with Republic Records, which was owned by Universal Music Group. With Republic, she released her seventh studio album, *Lover*, on August 23, 2019. Swift said that she wrote this album while she was in a good place in her life. The album reflects her happiness with songs such as "Lover," an ode to a successful relationship. It also includes "The Man," an exploration of society's double standards for women. Swift wrote *Lover*'s "You Need to Calm Down" in support of the LGBTQIA+ community. The music video features many queer celebrities and allies.

Around the same time, the 2020 presidential election was in full swing. Until the 2018 midterm elections, Swift had not publicly supported any candidates in an effort to avoid alienating any fans. But after endorsing Tennessee Democratic candidates in the midterm elections, she threw her support behind Democratic nominee Joseph Biden in the 2020 presidential election. She even allowed

Cat Lover

In December 2019, the musical movie *Cats* was released. Swift played the role of Bombalurina, a confident, striped cat. She performed the song "Macavity" using a British accent. Besides starring in the film, Swift teamed up with British composer Andrew Lloyd Webber to write the song "Beautiful Ghosts" for the film. In real life, Swift is a huge cat lover. She has three cats, Meredith Grey, Olivia Benson, and Benjamin Button.

Biden's campaign to use her song "Only the Young" for a commercial.

On January 31, 2020, Swift's fans got an intimate peek into her world when Netflix and select theaters released the documentary *Miss Americana.* It was filmed during Swift's Reputation Stadium Tour and while she wrote and released her *Lover* album. In the film, Swift revealed that after winning the Grammy for her album *1989*, she didn't have anyone to celebrate with but her mother. "She's my favorite person," Swift said of her mother. During the film, Swift's mother mentioned her battle with cancer. Andrea Swift has had breast cancer twice, and in 2019, she was diagnosed with a brain tumor.

Additionally, Swift shared her struggles with an eating disorder. She would strive to be thinner and would stop eating or exercise too much and sometimes faint. In the documentary, she advocated for eating healthfully. Swift also talked about her political activism and support of women's and LGBTQIA+ rights.

PaNDEMiC FiCTiON

During the pandemic, Swift sheltered at home and wrote her album *Folklore*, which she released on July 24, 2020. Swift wrote and recorded the songs in her home studio in Los Angeles, which she named Kitty Committee Studio after her three cats. Other artists contributed to the album remotely. With this album, Swift crossed into the indie

During the COVID-19 pandemic, people practiced social distancing to stay safe. Swift sang "Betty" at the 2020 Country Music Association Awards without an audience.

folk genre. According to Swiftie Olivia Montagno, "[Swift] hasn't pigeonholed herself in one genre. That is why she has transcended decades."

For *Folklore*, Swift moved away from writing lyrics that were based solely on her own experiences. Instead, she made up fictional characters and stories. The album includes songs such as "Cardigan," "Betty," and "August," which are about three young characters in a love triangle. Swift won her third Grammy for Album of the Year for *Folklore*. She is the first woman to win three of these awards, and one of only four artists to do so.

Swift filmed a documentary called *Folklore: The Long Pond Studio Sessions* at the Long Pond Studio in Columbia

County, New York. It was released on November 25, 2020. In the documentary, she sings all her songs from *Folklore*, accompanied by her coproducers Jack Antonoff and Aaron Dessner. Swift talks intimately about each song between performances. In these sessions, she reveals that her romantic partner at the time, British actor Joe Alwyn, was a contributing artist on the album. But to keep the collaboration private, he was listed under the pseudonym William Bowery.

Evermore is the sister album to *Folklore*. It was also written and produced during the pandemic. Swift said she "chose to wander deeper" into the music when writing this album. *Evermore* was released December 11, 2020. It includes the songs "Willow," "Champagne Problems," and "Marjorie," which recalls Swift's close relationship with her grandmother, Marjorie Finlay. Finlay's vocals are even used in the song.

Swift receiving the Grammy for Album of the Year for *Folklore* alongside coproducers Jack Antonoff (*middle*) and Aaron Dessner (*right*)

Swift released her tenth studio album, *Midnights*, on October 21, 2022. The album plays with the idea of color, with songs such as "Lavender Haze" and "Maroon." The album also includes the songs "You're on Your Own, Kid" and "Bejeweled," which celebrate female independence. With *Midnights*, Swift was the first artist to have ten songs in the top ten spots on the *Billboard* Hot 100 all at once.

Giving Back

Over the years, Swift has been involved with various charities and charity work. On October 13, 2011, she donated six thousand Scholastic children's books to her hometown's public library in Reading, Pennsylvania. Swift explained, "I wouldn't be a songwriter if it wasn't for books that I loved as a kid." Then, in 2021, Swift wrote a song called "Ronan" about a child with the same name, who had died of cancer just before his fourth birthday. The song was inspired by blog posts about Ronan, which were written by Ronan's mother, Maya Thompson. Swift credited Thompson as a cowriter on the song and gave all proceeds from it to cancer charities.

Swift singing on opening night of her Eras Tour at State Farm Stadium in Glendale, Arizona

THE ERaS TOUR

Swift kicked off the Eras Tour on March 17, 2023, in Glendale, Arizona. This energetic spectacle became the most successful musical tour in history, grossing more than $1 billion as of November 2023. The Eras Tour was so successful that Swift added more concert dates through December 2024. Wherever she brought the tour, the economy of that area thrived. Fans spent money on travel, hotels, restaurants, and stores, which benefited those places financially. This was called the Taylor effect.

The Taylor effect was helpful for craft stores. Swifties found a line about friendship bracelets in "You're on Your Own, Kid." They made beaded bracelets with words

Thirteen is Swift's favorite number. Swifties draw the number on their hands and wear friendship bracelets to her concerts.

on them to wear and share at concerts. The words might have been album titles or lyrics. Fans not only shared them with fellow Swifties but also with others, such as security guards who worked at the stadiums. One funny phrase found on some of the bracelets was "Starbucks Lovers." This was because a lyric from Swift's song "Blank Space" was often misheard. Even Swift's mom misheard the lyric!

Some wild things happened during the Eras Tour. When tickets first went on sale for the tour in 2022, the demand overwhelmed Ticketmaster's website, and it crashed. Over the course of the tour, fans who couldn't get tickets parked in nearby parking lots to hear the music. This was called Taylor-gating. Then there was the time the earth shook! Swift played at Lumen Field in Seattle, Washington, on July 22 and 23 in 2023. Between the huge crowd and performance onstage, the concert registered a 2.3 magnitude earthquake on the Richter scale. It was dubbed a Swift Quake.

Swift planned ways to make each concert date special for the audience. She would perform alone onstage, playing her guitar or piano. These intimate acoustic sets included different surprise songs at each concert. Swift also invited a surprise guest to perform with her at many of the concerts. For example, her friends Ed Sheeran and Selena Gomez joined her onstage. Swift also had rapper

Swift and Kelce

Dating rumors about Swift and Kansas City Chiefs tight end Travis Kelce began months before the two confirmed their relationship in fall 2023. The two often attend each other's events to show their support. Swift goes to many of Kelce's football games. Due to her appearances at these games, the Kansas City Chiefs have seen their own version of the Taylor effect. Swifties alone have generated over $300 million for the team. Kelce has been spotted at many of Swift's concerts, including one in Buenos Aires, Argentina, where he flew 5,000 miles (8,047 km) to see her perform.

Swift worked directly with AMC Theatres to release the film version of her Eras Tour in October 2023.

Ice Spice and indie-folk artist Phoebe Bridgers sing with her. Bridgers was even an opening act for Swift for some of the tour dates.

Then, on November 17, 2023, a tragic event occurred. At a concert in Rio de Janeiro, Brazil, a twenty-three-year-old woman died of heat-related injuries. The combined temperature and humidity that day made it feel as though it was 138°F (59°C). Many fans fainted. Some said that the organizers did not allow people to bring their own water into the venue. Other fans also noticed the air vents were blocked by boards to prevent people outside from enjoying the concert. Upon learning of the fan's tragic death, Swift said she had a "shattered heart." She canceled the concert scheduled for the next day to protect the audience.

For fans who were unable to see her concert in person or for those who wanted to experience it again, Swift released a film version of her concert called *Taylor Swift:*

The Eras Tour (Taylor's Version) on October 13, 2023. The movie was filmed during her August 2023 concerts at the SoFi Stadium in Inglewood, California. As of January 2024, the film was the highest-grossing concert or documentary film ever. It earned over $261 million.

SENSATIONAL SUCCESS

Swift took a break from touring in November 2023. She spent time with family and friends; attended Kansas City Chiefs football games to cheer on her boyfriend, Travis Kelce; and relaxed. Riding high on the success of the Eras Tour, Swift attended the Grammy Awards on February 4,

Swift attending a Kansas City Chiefs game during the 2023 National Football League regular season

Swift receives the Grammy Award for Best Pop Vocal Album in 2024.

2024. She won her fourth Grammy for Album of the Year for *Midnights.* She is the first person in history to win this award four times! In her acceptance speech, Swift said, "For me, the award is the work. . . . All I want to do is keep being able to do this [make music]."

On April 19, 2024, Swift released her eleventh studio album, *The Tortured Poets Department.* It is a secret double album, with thirty-one total songs. That's fifteen more tracks than fans were expecting! On the album, Swift includes the songs "Fortnight," with rapper Post Malone, and "So Long, London." Both songs are about difficult breakups. The album smashed records. On its first day of release, it sold 1.4 million copies. By the end of its first week, it had sold over 2.6 million copies, second only to Adele's *25.* Swift even broke her own record when fourteen songs from this album took the top fourteen spots on the *Billboard* Hot 100—all at the same time!

With eleven studio albums and fans across the globe, Taylor Swift's success is unquestionable. She has proven to be a skilled lyricist, singer, and musician. She is a smart businessperson, and her generosity toward others has made her popular with fans. Swift has accomplished so much. Swifties can't wait to see what comes next!

IMPORTANT DATES

1989	Taylor Swift is born in Reading, Pennsylvania, on December 13.
2005	Swift signs with Big Machine Records.
2006	Swift releases her first studio album, *Taylor Swift*.
2010	Swift wins her first Grammy for Album of the Year for *Fearless*.
2012	Swift releases music for the movie adaptation of *The Hunger Games*.
2016	Swift wins her second Grammy for Album of the Year for *1989*.
2018	Swift signs with Republic Records.

2020   *Folklore: The Long Pond Studio Sessions* film is released.

2021   Swift wins her third Grammy for Album of the Year for *Folklore*.

2023   Swift kicks off her Eras Tour in Glendale, Arizona.

Taylor Swift: The Eras Tour (Taylor's Version) movie is released.

2024   Swift wins her fourth Grammy for Album of the Year for *Midnights*.

Swift releases her eleventh studio album, *The Tortured Poets Department*.

SOURCE NOTES

7 Matt Fortin, "Swift Wows Fans during 3 Massive Shows at Gillette—Even Through Torrential Rain," 10 Boston, May 22, 2023, https://www.nbcboston.com/news/local/swift-wows-fans -during-3-massive-shows-at-gillette-even-through-torrential -rain/3050683/.

9 Nikki DeMentri, "Taylor Swift's Elementary School Teachers 'Beyond Proud' of Her Success," CBS News, April 20, 2024, https://www.cbsnews.com/philadelphia/news/taylor-swift -elementary-school-teachers-beyond-proud-berks-county -wyndcroft-school/.

10 Kate Morgan, "Taylor Swift's South Jersey Summers," *SJ Magazine*, May 2023, https://sjmagazine.net/featured/taylor -swifts-south-jersey-summers.

11–12 Chris Willman, "Taylor Swift's Road to Fame," *Entertainment Weekly*, February 5, 2008, https://ew.com/article/2008/02/05 /taylor-swifts-road-fame/.

15 Jack Dickey, "The Power of Taylor Swift," *Time*, November 13, 2014, https://time.com/3583129/power-of-taylor-swift-cover/.

16 Samantha Neely and Lianna Norman, "Taylor Swift Fans Find Clues Tied to Florida Ahead of 'The Tortured Poet's Department' Release," *Florida Today*, updated April 19, 2024, https:// www.floridatoday.com/story/news/2024/04/18/taylor-swift -florida-tortured-poets-department-album-release/73367248007/.

31 *Miss Americana*, directed by Lana Wilson, Netflix, 2020, https://
www.netflix.com/title/81028336.

32 Olivia and Gianna Montagno, interview with the author,
April 25, 2024.

33 Raisa Bruner, "Let's Break Down Taylor Swift's New Album
Evermore," *Time*, December 11, 2020, https://time.com/5920105
/taylor-swift-evermore/.

34 Megan Kaesshaefer, "Happening TODAY: An Exclusive Video
with Taylor Swift!," Scholastic, October 29, 2014, https://
oomscholasticblog.com/post/happening-today-exclusive-video
-taylor-swift.

38 Reuters, "Taylor Swift Fan Died of Heat Exhaustion at Rio
Concert, Brazilian Police Say," NBC News, December 27, 2023,
https://www.nbcnews.com/news/world/taylor-swift-eras-tour
-brazil-fan-died-heat-exhaustion-rcna131296.

41 Douglas Markowitz, "2024 Grammys: Taylor Swift Makes
Grammy History with Fourth Album of the Year Win for
'Midnights,'" Grammy Awards, February 4, 2024, https://
www.grammy.com/news/taylor-swift-album-of-the-year-2024
-grammys-speech.

SELECTED BIBLIOGRAPHY

Carlin, Shannon. "A Very Good Year." *Time Special Edition Taylor Swift: A Magical Era*, November 2023, 5–7.

Dickey, Jack. "An All-American Voice." *Time Special Edition Taylor Swift: A Magical Era*, November 2023, 27–38.

Driessen, Simone. "Campaign Problems: How Fans React to Taylor Swift's Controversial Political Awakening." *American Behavioral Scientist* 66, no. 8 (March 22, 2022). https://journals.sagepub.com/doi/10.1177/00027642211042295.

Folklore: The Long Pond Studio Sessions. Directed by Taylor Swift. Disney+, 2020. https://www.disneyplus.com/movies/folklore-the-long-pond-studio-sessions/3XlcOEjKtKpp.

Lansky, Sam. "2023 Person of the Year: Taylor Swift." *Time*, December 6, 2023. https://time.com/6342806/person-of-the-year-2023-taylor-swift/.

Miss Americana. Directed by Lana Wilson. Netflix, 2020. https://www.netflix.com/title/81028336.

"Swift." Pennsylvania Center for the Book. Accessed June 4, 2024. https://pabook.libraries.psu.edu/swift__taylor/.

"Taylor Swift Biography." IMDb. Accessed June 21, 2024. https://www.imdb.com/name/nm2357847/bio/.

Taylor Swift: The Eras Tour (Taylor's Version). Directed by Sam Wrench. Disney+, 2024. https://www.disneyplus.com/movies/taylor-swift-the-eras-tour-taylors-version/OHLx94HKtS6X.

LEARN MORE

Anderson, Kirsten. *Who Is Taylor Swift?* New York: Penguin Workshop, 2024.

Britannica: Taylor Swift
https://www.britannica.com/biography/Taylor-Swift

Cooke, Tim. *Taylor Swift and Paul McCartney: Legendary Songwriters.* Minneapolis: Lerner Publications, 2025.

Kiddle: Taylor Swift Facts for Kids
https://kids.kiddle.co/Taylor_Swift

Nnachi, Ngeri. *Changemakers in Music: Women Leading the Way.* Minneapolis: Lerner Publications, 2024.

Rose, Rachel. *Taylor Swift: Singer, Songwriter, and Activist.* Minneapolis: Bearport, 2023.

Time for Kids: A Taylor-Made Star
https://www.timeforkids.com/g56/taylor-made-star-2/

Time for Kids: The Taylor Effect
https://www.timeforkids.com/g34/taylor-effect-g3/?rl=en-630

INDEX

PHOTO ACKNOWLEDGMENTS

Image credits: TAS Rights Management/Getty Images, pp. 2, 6; Charles McQuillan/TAS24/Getty Images, p. 8; Rick Diamond/Getty Images for CMT, p. 11; Michael Caulfield/WireImage, p. 13; John Shearer/Getty Images for 13 Management, p. 14; Kevin Winter/Getty Images, p. 15; Michael Loccisano/FilmMagic, p. 16; Rick Diamond/WireImage, p. 17; Jason Kempin/Getty Images, p. 18; Jon Kopaloff/FilmMagic, p. 19; AP Photo/Matt Sayles, p. 20; Larry Busacca/Getty Images, p. 21; Joel Ryan/Invision/AP, p. 23; Scott Weiner/MediaPunch /IPX, p. 24; Charles Sykes/Invision/AP, p. 25; Taylor Hill/FilmMagic, p. 28; TASRIGHTSMANAGEMENT2020/Getty Images, p. 32; Kevin Winter/Getty Images for The Recording Academy, pp. 33, 35; Gary Coronado/Los Angeles Times via Getty Images, p. 36; Barry King/Alamy, p. 38; David Eulitt/Getty Images, p. 39; AP Photo/Chris Pizzello, p. 40. Cover: NurPhoto SRL/Alamy.